BOSNIA AND HERZEGOVINA: HUMAN RIGHTS

EXECUTIVE SUMMARY

Bosnia and Herzegovina (BiH) is a democratic republic with a bicameral parliament but assigns many governmental functions to two entities within the state, the Federation of Bosnia and Herzegovina (the Federation) and the Republika Srpska (RS), and to the Brcko District, an independent administrative unit under the sovereignty of BiH. The 1995 General Framework Agreement for Peace (the Dayton Accords), which ended the 1992-95 Bosnian war, provides the constitutional framework for governmental structures while other parts of the agreement specify the government's obligations to ensure human rights, such as guaranteeing the right of persons displaced by the war to return to their prewar homes. The Dayton Accords also provide for a high representative who has the authority to impose legislation and remove officials. In 2010 the country held general elections that international observers deemed free and fair. The coalitions formed at the state and Federation levels following those elections remained unstable, with regular efforts to change the coalitions' composition preventing political progress. Authorities failed at times to maintain effective control over security forces. Security forces did not commit widespread or systemic human rights abuses.

Government corruption and dysfunction remained among the country's most serious problems and impeded citizens' rights to basic services, including access to necessary travel documents. This prompted protests in June, the largest demonstrations in the country since independence. Political leaders intensified and manipulated deep-seated ethnic divisions that weakened democracy and governance, fostered widespread discrimination in most aspects of daily life, undermined the rule of law, distorted public discourse in the media, and obstructed the return of persons displaced by the 1992-95 conflict. Harassment and intimidation of journalists and civil society limited the public's access to accurate information and accountability of political leaders.

Other human rights problems included: deaths from land mines; police mistreatment of suspects during questioning; harsh conditions in prisons and detention centers, such as overcrowding and physical abuse of prisoners and detainees; police failure to inform detainees of their rights or allow effective access to legal counsel prior to questioning; failure to return properties to religious communities; discrimination and violence against women and members of sexual and religious minorities; discrimination against persons with disabilities; trafficking in persons; and limits on employment rights.

Both entities and the Brcko District maintained units that investigated allegations of police abuses, meted out administrative penalties, and referred cases of criminal misconduct to prosecutors. These units generally operated effectively, and there were no reports of impunity during the year.

Section 1. Respect for the Integrity of the Person, Including Freedom from:

a. Arbitrary or Unlawful Deprivation of Life

There were no reports that the government or its agents committed arbitrary or unlawful killings.

Despite local and international efforts to prosecute war crimes, many lower-ranking perpetrators remained unpunished, including those responsible for the approximately 8,000 persons killed in the Srebrenica genocide and those responsible for approximately 9,000 other persons who were missing and presumed killed during the 1992-95 war. Implementation of the *National Strategy for Processing War Crimes* was slow, reflecting the complexity of cases and the dearth of budget and personnel support extended to the state, entity, district, and cantonal courts and prosecutor's offices. During the year the Organization for Security and Cooperation in Europe (OSCE) provided new financial assistance to facilitate implementation of the strategy.

The *National Strategy for Processing War Crimes* foresees the prosecution of the most complex war crimes cases by 2016 and all other war crimes cases by 2024. The International Criminal Tribunal for the former Yugoslavia was processing the remaining cases in its jurisdiction arising from killings during the 1992-95 conflict. The Bosnia and Herzegovina Court War Crimes Chamber and entity courts also continued war crimes trials during the year, albeit at a very slow pace because of delays associated with identifying and preparing witnesses for testimony, availability of courtrooms, and a lack of prosecutorial capacity at the entity level. In addition, the local practice of noncontinuous trials, at which a small part of a case was heard once per week at most, created lengthy delays in trial proceedings. Nevertheless, the country made progress in implementing the national war crimes strategy following the referrals of many cases from the national to entity-level courts.

On September 6, the Dutch Supreme Court ruled that the Government of The Netherlands was liable for the deaths of three Bosniaks killed in 1995 in Srebrenica. The men had sought shelter in the UN camp controlled by Dutch peacekeepers under UN command, but the peacekeepers forced them to leave, and Bosnian Serb forces subsequently killed them. The ruling was the first in which a court held a foreign government accountable for the actions of its forces under UN command in Bosnia.

During the year eight land mine accidents injured 10 persons and killed three. The country has a demining strategy, but it remained largely unfunded. According to the country's Mine Action Center, there are still more than 9,555 active minefields (with an estimated 120,000 devices) endangering an estimated 540,000 residents throughout the country at year's end. In many cases the presence of land mines slowed the return of internally displaced persons and the exhumation of mass graves.

b. Disappearance

There were no reports of politically motivated disappearances.

c. Torture and Other Cruel, Inhuman, or Degrading Treatment or Punishment

The law prohibits such practices. The Council of Europe's Committee for the Prevention of Torture (CPT) reported, however, that police mistreatment of detainees at times "was of such severity that it would amount to torture."

On September 12, the CPT released the report on its December 2012 visit to RS police and remand detention centers. The CPT delegation reported a considerable number of credible allegations of serious physical mistreatment by law enforcement officials in the RS, including slaps, punches, kicks, use of small handheld electroshock devices, handcuffing in stress positions for long periods, using plastic bags over the heads of suspects, and beatings with hard objects, including baseball bats. Several detainees stated that police had subjected them to mock execution with a pistol pointed at their temple or inserted into their mouth and the trigger pulled. The majority of abuses allegedly occurred during police efforts to obtain confessions from suspects during questioning.

Prison and Detention Center Conditions

Conditions in the country's prisons and detention centers were harsh and, on occasion, life threatening. Prisons had wholly inadequate sanitation and medical care.

Physical Conditions: At the end of September there were 4,200 persons incarcerated in the country). The government estimated the total capacity of Federation and RS prisons at 3,217 persons. Some prisons in the country remained overcrowded.

During the year there was one recorded death of an inmate at Zenica Prison. Police and the Prosecutor's Office promptly launched an investigation of the case, which was still underway in September. Prisoners had access to adequate potable water, but poor hygiene and antiquated facilities remained serious problems.

During prison visits to Mostar, Trebinje, Zenica, Banja Luka, Bihac, Doboj, Orasje, Foca, Tuzla, and Bijeljina during the year, the state-level parliament's Commission for Monitoring Conditions in Prisons noted a lack of health care professionals and the need to decrease wait times for routine medical examinations. In many cases, budgetary considerations appeared to outweigh concern for prisoner hygiene. The commission called on the government to provide the financial means necessary to reduce overcrowding by focusing on reconstruction of old prisons, building new prisons, and hiring additional staff.

The commission criticized the prison in Zenica for overcrowding, inadequate conditions for women, and lack of basic social services for persons with mental disabilities. Specifically the commission reported that two-person cells did not have separate bathrooms, prison management did not provide separate cells for men and women, and inmates with mental disabilities lacked access to qualified medical personnel. In Trebinje the commission found that prisoners lacked access to bathroom facilities for extended periods because the prison rarely allowed prisoners to leave their cells and bathrooms are located outside of cells.

Administration: There were reports of delays by law enforcement agencies in keeping records of arrests prior to the transfer of arrested persons to a prosecutor's office. In the report on its 2012 visit, the CPT delegation noted serious shortfalls in recording injuries sustained by detainees. The CPT attributed this in part to authorities' frequently denying detainees access to medical treatment with law enforcement officers present. As of September, the RS Ministry of Justice had not taken measures to address the CPT's findings. The law does allow alternatives to incarceration, including community service and electronic monitoring devices, such as ankle bracelets. Authorities used parole in accordance with the law.

The law allows detainees and prisoners to send requests or complaints to the country's ombudsman, who has authority to advocate for the rights of prisoners, including juveniles, regarding status and circumstances of confinement, bail, overcrowding, and other conditions. The ombudsman also can advocate on behalf of prisoners to improve pretrial conditions and recordkeeping to reduce the incidence of prisoners serving beyond their maximum sentences. The ombudsman lacked authority to advocate for alternatives to incarceration for nonviolent offenders to alleviate overcrowding. There were no reports that prison authorities failed to forward requests from inmates to the ombudsman.

Authorities permitted prisoners and detainees access to visitors and religious observance. The law provides for the right of prisoners to communicate, file complaints, and expect expeditious resolution of violations, and authorities generally investigated credible allegations of inhuman conditions.

Independent Monitoring: The government permitted independent human rights observers to visit and gave international community representatives widespread and unhindered access to detention facilities and prisoners.

The International Committee of the Red Cross (ICRC) continued to have access to detention facilities under the jurisdiction of the ministries of justice at both the state and entity levels.

Improvements: State-level authorities were building a prison to reduce overcrowding that was scheduled for completion in 2015. In East Sarajevo, the prison for women added a section.

d. Arbitrary Arrest or Detention

The law prohibits arbitrary arrest and detention, and the government generally observed these prohibitions.

Role of the Police and Security Apparatus

The law extends significant overlapping law enforcement competencies to the state-level government, each entity, and the Brcko District, each of which has its own police force. An EU military force continued to support the country's government in maintaining a safe and secure environment for the population. A NATO headquarters in Sarajevo continued to assist the country's authorities in the implementation of defense reform and counterterrorism.

Civilian authorities maintained effective control over security forces. By law the two entities, the Brcko District, and 10 cantonal interior ministries exercise police powers. The State Investigation and Protection Agency (SIPA) facilitates regional cooperation in combating organized crime, human trafficking, and international terrorism. State border police are responsible for monitoring the borders and for the detention of irregular migrants. The Department for Police Coordination provides security for government and diplomatic buildings and protection for state-level officials and visiting dignitaries.

The government has effective mechanisms to investigate and punish abuse and corruption; however, political pressure often prevented the use of these mechanisms. While there were no reports of impunity during the year, there were continued reports of corruption within the entity- and state-level security services. Professional standards units are the internal affairs investigative units in each entity's interior ministry and in the Brcko District. Throughout the year, mostly with assistance from the international community, the government provided training to police and security forces designed to combat abuse and corruption and promote respect for human rights.

Arrest Procedures and Treatment of Detainees

Police generally arrested persons with warrants based on sufficient evidence. The law requires authorities to inform detainees of the charges against them immediately upon first questioning and police to bring suspects before a prosecutor within 24 hours of detention. During this period police may detain individuals for up to six hours at the scene of a crime for investigative purposes. The prosecutor has an additional 24 hours to release the person or to request a court order extending pretrial detention. There is a functioning bail system, and the law provides for the right to a speedy trial.

The law allows detainees to request a lawyer of their own choosing. In the report on its 2012 visit to RS detention facilities, the CPT noted that RS authorities frequently did not respect a suspect's right to counsel and that a suspect's first encounter with legal counsel was generally at the time of his or her first court appearance and after long periods of coercive interrogation. Many persons complained that lawyers provided by authorities remained silent throughout the initial court proceedings.

There were no reports that authorities detained suspects incommunicado or held them improperly under house arrest.

Pretrial Detention: Lengthy pretrial detention was generally not a problem. The law limits pretrial detention to one year and sets strict limits on the duration of custody during both the pre-indictment phase and after indictment. In order for custody to be continued, a court must review the case at regularly prescribed intervals. Defendants have the right to appeal detention.

e. Denial of Fair Public Trial

The state constitution does not explicitly provide for an independent judiciary, but the laws of both entities do. Political parties and organized crime figures sometimes influenced the judiciary at both the state and entity levels in politically sensitive cases.

The country's criminal code criminalizes failure to enforce decisions of the country's Constitutional Court, the Court of Bosnia and Herzegovina, and the European Court of Human Rights (ECHR). There were numerous instances in which legislative and executive authorities at the national or entity level did not fully implement the Constitutional Court's decisions. After exhausting all domestic legal measures, plaintiffs often brought these cases before the ECHR to enforce compliance. According to the 2012 *European Court BiH Progress Report*, there were 1,433 applications pending before the ECHR against the state.

Trial Procedures

The law provides that defendants enjoy a presumption of innocence, the right to be informed promptly and in detail of the charges against them with free interpretation if necessary, and the right to a fair and public trial without undue delay. The law does not provide for trial by jury. The law provides for the right to counsel at public expense if the prosecutor charges the defendant with a serious crime. Courts did not always appoint defense attorneys where the maximum prison sentence was less than five years. Authorities generally gave defense attorneys adequate time and facilities to prepare their clients' defenses. The law provides defendants the right to confront witnesses, to present witnesses and evidence on their own behalf, to access government-held evidence relevant to their case, and to appeal verdicts. Authorities generally respected most of these rights.

The state-level prosecutor's office continued to use plea agreements in some cases.

Political Prisoners and Detainees

There were no reports of political prisoners or detainees.

Civil Judicial Procedures and Remedies

The law provides for individuals and organizations to seek civil remedies for human rights violations and provides for the appeal of decisions to the ECHR. The government failed to comply with many domestic and regional court decisions pertaining to human rights.

The court system suffered from large backlogs of cases and the lack of an effective mechanism to enforce court orders. Inefficiency in the courts undermined the rule of law by making recourse to civil judgments less effective. The government's failure to comply with court decisions has led plaintiffs to bring 1,433 cases before the ECHR after exhausting all legal measures domestically.

Regional Human Rights Court Decisions

The country is a party to the European Convention on Human Rights and subject to the jurisdiction of the ECHR. The country complied with ECHR judgments requiring individual measures, either through actual remedies or by submitting action plans for compliance to the ECHR. It remained noncompliant, however, with the ECHR's 2009 Sejdic-Finci judgment that the country's constitutional provisions on ethnic minorities' running for certain elected offices violated the European Convention on Human Rights.

As of September there were 1,433 cases before the ECHR against the state for alleged failure to comply with numerous domestic court decisions pertaining to human rights, including problems concerning missing persons, old currency savings, and compensation for war damages.

Property Restitution

The country's four traditional religious communities had extensive claims for restitution of property nationalized during and after World War II. Many officials used property restitution cases to provide political patronage. In a few cases government officials refused to return properties legally recognized as belonging to religious institutions. In July progress was made on a 2010 agreement to return a building that houses the University of Sarajevo's economics faculty to the Serbian Orthodox Church, whose ownership of the building had been legally recognized before the 1992-95 conflict. The Sarajevo canton prime minister, the minister of education, and the dean of the Orthodox theological faculty in Foca, as well as the deans of the economics faculty, the Roman Catholic theological faculty, and the Islamic theological faculty in Sarajevo, signed a memorandum of understanding establishing the Institute for the Study of Inter-Religious Dialogue in the building. The Serbian Orthodox faculty in Foca is scheduled to run the institute out of one room of the economics faculty, thus representing an important first step towards a full return of ownership to the Serb Orthodox Church.

Roma displaced during the 1992-95 conflict had difficulty repossessing their property as a result of discrimination and because they lacked documents proving ownership or had never registered their property with local authorities.

f. Arbitrary Interference with Privacy, Family, Home, or Correspondence

The law prohibits such actions, and the government generally respected these prohibitions.

Section 2. Respect for Civil Liberties, Including:

a. Freedom of Speech and Press

The law provides for freedom of speech and press, but the government did not always respect press freedom. Laws delegated safeguarding freedom of the press to the cantons in the Federation and to the entity-level authorities in the RS. Government respect for freedom of speech and the press continued to deteriorate during the year.

Freedom of Speech: The RS government continued to discourage political expression. During the year the RS government submitted a report to the RS National Assembly criticizing protest activities in social media and alleging that individuals with Bosniak names were particularly active on internet forums and Facebook. In June RS President Milorad Dodik accused the state-level public broadcaster BHT and other media outlets of instigative and politically motivated reporting related to the June protests. Specifically, Dodik accused BHT of encouraging the citizens of Banja Luka to protest through social media.

Federation law prohibits hate speech. RS law does not specifically proscribe hate speech, although the law prohibits causing ethnic, racial, or religious hatred. Many media outlets used incendiary language, often nationalistic, with impunity on matters related to ethnicity, religion, and political affiliation. Additionally, lesbian, gay, bisexual, and transgender (LGBT) activists came under frequent attack in the media often using homophobic language.

As of September the Communications Regulatory Agency (CRA) registered one case of hate speech during the year. During an April episode of TV Pink's program *Forbidden Forum* on the subject of same-sex marriage, hate speech was found in text messages from audience members that were broadcast on the show. The station was fined 4,000 convertible marks ($ 2,800). The Press Council of Bosnia and Herzegovina registered 20 cases of incitement and spread-of-hate speech from January to the end of August, all referring to online media.

Independent analysts noted the continuing tendency of politicians and other leaders to label unwanted criticism as hate speech.

Press Freedoms: The independent media were active and expressed a wide variety of views but were subject to excessive influence from government, political parties, and private interest groups. The media divided reporting along political and ethnic lines. Public broadcasters at the state and entity levels continued to face strong political pressure from entity governments and political forces that consistently threatened the independence of public broadcasters and led to consistently unobjective and politically tainted news. Both entity governments financially supported news agencies that they viewed favorably. Unlike previous years, there were no reports that the RS government provided any direct budgetary support to media outlets beyond subsidies allocated in 2012 that it provided early in the year.

State-level authorities continued attempts to weaken the CRA by injecting partisan politics into the organization's oversight and management and diminishing the organization's regulatory powers. The law empowers the CRA to regulate all aspects of the country's audiovisual market, including broadcast media.

In April the state-level parliament selected six candidates, which included two nongovernmental representatives only after strong public criticism, for an ad hoc committee to select the CRA's governing council. The process of selecting the CRA's governing council was underway during the year.

Authorities continued their efforts to appoint multiple members to the Federation Radio and Television (FTV) steering board, despite a legal requirement that only one member of the steering board may be appointed in any single calendar year, and completed accepting applications for new members despite procedural irregularities. In March the Federation parliament approved the proposal of its Committee for Information to form a new temporary steering board, which runs contrary to CRA regulations. Parliament did not adopt the decision because a number of delegates from the Federation parliament invoked vital national interest, a voting mechanism that prevented further consideration on the matter. The legality of the appointment of the temporary steering board was under review by the Federation's Constitutional Court. In October the Republika Srpska National Assembly (RSNA) adopted amendments to the Law on Radio Television of the RS (RTRS) allowing the entity government to finance the RTRS directly. The law also mandates that the RSNA appoint members of the RTRS steering board, which is contrary to the regulatory powers delegated to the CRA.

Institutional instability within the governing structures of the FTV and the RTRS made the public broadcaster vulnerable to continued political pressure. This was further exacerbated by state-level authorities' failure to establish a single steering board to oversee the operations of all public broadcasters in the country as required by law and a reduction of advertising time from six to four minutes per hour, which threatened the financial stability of public broadcasters. In response, the international community, including the EU, repeatedly raised concerns about attempts by authorities to undercut the responsibilities of public broadcasters by emphasizing the need to harmonize legislation with the regulatory powers of the CRA.

Many privately owned newspapers were available and expressed a wide variety of views. A number of independent print media outlets continued to encounter financial problems that endangered their operations.

Violence and Harassment: During the year there were credible reports of intimidation of and politically motivated litigation against journalists for unfavorable reporting on government leaders and authorities. The Free Media Help Line registered 37 cases involving violations of journalists' rights and freedoms or pressure from government and law enforcement officials. There were 14 cases of pressure on and threats against journalists, including two death threats and two physical attacks; other cases involved denial of access to information. In September there was an alleged arson attempt at the headquarters of *Slobodna Bosna,* a daily print media outlet based in Sarajevo that was known for its investigative reporting. The editorial board and independent analysts believed this was an attempt to intimidate the outlet's investigative reporters. The Sarajevo Police Department opened an investigation into the incident.

Censorship or Content Restrictions: Some political parties attempted to influence editorial policies and media content through legal and financial measures. As a result, some media outlets practiced self-censorship.

In some instances media sources reported that officials threatened outlets with loss of advertising or limited their access to official information. Editors and journalists from RTV Una Sana canton sought assistance from the BiH Journalists' Association in response to political pressure from the mayor of Bihac, who allegedly called on public institutions and public companies to boycott the cantonal television station. The Free Media Help Line reported that it received similar complaints of political pressure from RTV Gorazde, RTV Tuzla Canton, and other public media outlets operating at the local level.

Internet Freedom

There were no government restrictions on access to the internet. During the year there were reports that the RS monitored internet activities on sites such as Facebook and Twitter. Following large-scale protests in front of the state-level parliament in June, which organizers facilitated largely through social media, the RS Ministry of Interior stated publicly that it had begun monitoring Facebook and Twitter in order to take necessary actions against future demonstrations. When civil society organizations protested the move, the ministry confirmed that it was monitoring internet activities as part of its regular law enforcement activities. According to the 2012 annual Communications Regulatory Agency report published in May, an estimated 57 percent of the population used the internet in 2012.

Academic Freedom and Cultural Events

There were no government restrictions on academic freedom or cultural events.

In Sarajevo, Serbs and Croats complained that Bosniaks received preferential treatment in appointments and promotions at the University of Sarajevo. The University of Banja Luka and the University of East Sarajevo continued to limit faculty appointments almost exclusively to Serbs, although some colleges expanded cooperation and exchanges of faculty members with their Federation counterparts during the year.

b. Freedom of Peaceful Assembly and Association

Freedom of Assembly

The law provides for freedom of assembly, and the government generally respected this right.

In June individuals gathered in front of the state-level parliament to protest government inaction on a law for issuing personal identification numbers and other problems affecting citizens' access to social services. The protests, which began June 4 and grew to a crowd estimated at 26,000 on June 11, were peaceful and members of all ethnic groups participated.

Freedom of Association

The law provides for freedom of association, and the government generally respected this right, although some nongovernmental organizations (NGOs) reported difficulty registering. While the law allows NGOs to register freely, some NGOs and NGO associations experienced long delays and inconsistent application of the law. Some NGOs, frustrated by delays at the state level, chose instead to register their organizations at the entity level.

c. Freedom of Religion

See the Department of State's *International Religious Freedom Report* at www.state.gov/j/drl/irf/rpt.

d. Freedom of Movement, Internally Displaced Persons, Protection of Refugees, and Stateless Persons

While the law provides for freedom of internal movement, foreign travel, emigration, and repatriation, and the government mostly respected these rights, some restrictions remained. The RS Ministry for Refugees and Displaced Persons and the Federation Ministry for Refugees worked independently and in collaboration with each other and the State Commission for Refugees to provide support to returnees, such as limited reconstruction assistance. The government cooperated with the Office of the UN High Commissioner for Refugees (UNHCR) and other humanitarian organizations in providing protection and assistance to internally displaced persons, refugees, returning refugees, asylum seekers, stateless persons, and other persons of concern.

Internally Displaced Persons (IDPs)

During the 1992-95 Bosnian War approximately one million individuals became IDPs. The majority of Bosniaks and Croats fled Republika Srpska, while Serbs fled the Federation. According to the UNHCR, an estimated 8,600 persons, mostly IDPs, continued to live in collective accommodations, meant to be temporary, 20 years after the war. Collective accommodations were located throughout the country._Many of the IDPs were so-called difficult cases, persons with mental disabilities, old, or chronically ill and in urgent need of assistance. Government officials and some NGOs believed that the actual number of persons who returned to their prewar communities was significantly lower than the UNHRC estimated, since the UNHCR determined returns based on property restitution rather than physical presence.

The Dayton Peace Accords provide for the right of return to their homes of persons displaced in the war. The country's constitution and laws provide for the voluntary return or resettlement of IDPs consistent with the UN Guiding Principles on Internal Displacement.

High rates of unemployment, lack of access to social benefits, lack of housing, and high municipal administration taxes on documents necessary to apply for reconstruction assistance continued to inhibit the return of IDPs. Minority returnees often faced intimidation, discrimination in hiring, and obstructions in their access to education, health care, and pension benefits, as well as poor infrastructure. There were also reports of attacks on minority religious sites as well as reports that the RS government deregistered the residences of potential Bosniak returnees to the RS, effectively inhibiting or preventing their return and/or political participation upon return.

During the year ethnic Bosniaks seeking to return to their prewar community of Srebrenica continued to complain that RS authorities attempted to prevent them from registering to vote by insisting that they provide, at their expense, documents beyond those required by election law. Following the October 2012 local elections, RS authorities questioned the organizers of the Bosniak registration drive about their activities. The organizers viewed this as harassment and an attempt to stifle political participation.

State- and entity-level laws provide for the protection of displaced persons, as well as returnees, in accordance with the UN Guiding Principles on Internal Displacement.

There were no legal restrictions on IDP access to humanitarian organizations and assistance, but application procedures were complicated, and some IDPs often could not afford to pay the costs associated with an application for assistance.

Protection of Refugees

Access to Asylum: The country's laws provide for the granting of asylum or refugee status; however, the system for providing protection to refugees suffered from a lack of transparency during the year. Asylum seekers with pending claims, regardless of national origin, could remain in asylum centers until the Ministry of Security adjudicated their claims, a process that normally took three months or longer. In urgent cases concerning manifestly unfounded claims, the process took 15 days. Asylum seekers have the right to appeal a negative decision within 60 days in regular procedure cases and within eight days in urgent cases. In urgent cases, a court is required to render a decision within 30 days. According to the UNHCR, during the year many asylum seekers were denied full refugee status by the Ministry of Security without explanation, and detention of asylum seekers for periods of more than six months became increasingly prevalent.

Safe Country of Origin/Transit: The law provides for the application of the concept of "safe country of origin," and claims of asylum seekers coming from a "safe country of origin" are considered unfounded. Under the law an asylum applicant must prove that the country is not safe for him or her.

Employment: Asylum seekers do not have the right to employment until the government grants them asylum.

Durable Solutions: Along with Serbia, Croatia, and Montenegro, the country is party to a regional refugee agreement and regional housing program (RHP) facilitated by the UNHCR and the OSCE to provide durable solutions for up to 74,000 refugees and displaced persons from the four partner countries, including

14,000 most vulnerable refugees, returnees, and IDPs from Bosnia. In April 2012 the country hosted an international donors' conference that raised approximately 207 million convertible marks ($300 million) to assist those refugees. Projects specific to Bosnia were approved by the RHP donors in April, and construction of housing projects was scheduled to begin in early 2014.

Temporary Protection: During the year the government did not grant temporary protection to any individuals not considered to qualify as refugees. The government, however, did extend subsidiary protection to 20 Syrians, five Bangladeshis, and five individuals from various countries in the Horn of Africa. Subsidiary protection in the country does not allow asylum seekers to obtain documents for international travel, reunify with family from abroad, or benefit from state social services.

Stateless Persons

The law provides that a child born to one or two parents who are citizens of the country is also a citizen, regardless of the place of birth. A child born on the territory of the country to parents who are not citizens does not gain citizenship unless both parents are stateless persons.

According to the UNHCR, more than 4,500 persons, the large majority of them Roma, were at risk of statelessness at year's end. This figure included persons whose births were not registered as well as persons at risk of denaturalization (largely those whom authorities naturalized during the 1992-95 conflict).

While the law provides no special provisions to expedite naturalization for stateless persons, it provides stateless persons opportunities to gain nationality on a nondiscriminatory basis. Stateless persons apply for naturalization through the same procedures as other foreigners.

During the year persons in need of documentation, and consequently at risk of statelessness, faced obstacles in the form of bureaucratic requirements to complete birth and civil registration as well as inefficient registration procedures.

While there were no reports of discrimination against persons at risk of statelessness, those at risk overwhelmingly were members of the Romani minority who faced discrimination in employment, education, housing, health services, marriage, birth registration, access to courts/judicial procedures, and land and property ownership based on their ethnicity.

Section 3. Respect for Political Rights: The Right of Citizens to Change Their Government

The law provides citizens with the right to change their government peacefully, and citizens exercised this right through periodic multi-party elections based on universal suffrage.

Elections and Political Participation

Recent Elections: Observers from the OSCE concluded that the 2010 general election was largely conducted in line with international standards but noted problems, including deficiencies in the registration process, group voting, and irregularities in the counting process. The OSCE observation mission noted that private media, particularly print media, tended to favor certain candidates. Smaller parties complained of systematic underexposure in the media.

Political Parties: The law does not restrict the formation of or participation in political parties. Some leaders of smaller political parties complained that the larger parties enjoyed a virtual monopoly over government ministries, public services, and media outlets.

Participation of Women and Minorities: The law requires that at least 30 percent of political party candidates be women. Nine of 42 members of the state-level House of Representatives were women. There were no women in the 10-member Council of Ministers, although there were six female deputy ministers. At the entity level, one woman was a minister in the Federation government and another a deputy speaker in parliament. Following the 2010 elections, 22 women were elected to the 98-member Federation House of Representatives and 14 to the 58-member Federation House of Peoples. In the RS, five of 16 ministers, including the prime minister and one deputy speaker in parliament, were women. Women held 18 of 83 seats in the RS National Assembly. In the RS Council of Peoples, women held four of 28 seats. During the year women parliamentarians formed a caucus in the Federation House of Representatives, the first formal, intraparty grouping in any legislature in the country.

The law provides that Serbs, Croats, and Bosniaks, whom the constitution considers the "constituent peoples" of the country, and "others" must be adequately represented in entity, cantonal, and municipal government institutions, based on the 1991 census, until the returns process detailed by the Dayton Accords is completed. The government did not respect this law. Separate from the three constituent peoples, there were 16 recognized national minority groups. Minorities not regarded as "constituent peoples" under the country's constitution remained severely underrepresented in government. There were no members of a minority group in the state-level parliament and only one member in the Council of Ministers, the child of an ethnically mixed marriage who declined to identify with a specific group.

In 2009 the ECHR ruled in the "Sejdic-Finci" case that the country's constitution discriminates against so-called others, such as Jews and Roma, because it prevents them from running for the presidency and seats in parliament's upper house. During the year the government failed to implement the ruling. The Council of Europe and the EU warned that failure to implement the ruling before the 2014 elections would call into question the legitimacy and credibility of those bodies.

Section 4. Corruption and Lack of Transparency in Government

The law provides for criminal penalties for official corruption, but the government did not implement the law effectively. Government officials frequently engaged in corrupt practices with impunity and corruption remained prevalent in many political and economic institutions in the country. The public viewed corruption as endemic in the public sphere. The multitude of state, entity, cantonal, and municipal administrations, each with the power to establish laws and regulations affecting business, created a system that lacked transparency and provided opportunities for corruption. With the large number of levels involved, there were multiple opportunities to demand "service fees."

Corruption: Professors and students reported that corruption at government institutions in secondary education was routine. The grading system, in which a professor (who may not be the instructor) assigns a grade and signs his or her name on the student's report card, was not transparent and often opened the door to corruption. Professors at a number of universities reported that bribery was common and that they experienced pressure from colleagues and superiors to give higher grades to students with family or political connections.

In April Zivko Budimir, president of the Federation entity, was arrested by SIPA on orders from the Prosecutor's Office based on allegations of abuse of office, specifically for allegedly selling pardons. A court ordered Budmir, who did not have criminal immunity, held for 30 days, but an appellate court ruled that the order was improper, and he was released. During a search of his office, SIPA found an unregistered weapon and Budimir was charged with illegal possession of the weapon, a misdemeanor offense. He failed to appear at an August 30 hearing on the case, citing a medical emergency. The case remained ongoing.

The state-level government formed an anticorruption agency during the year, but it was not included in the annual budget. Nevertheless, the agency operated on minimal state funds. The agency is responsible for investigating and prosecuting corruption cases.

During the year the state-level prosecutor's office referred several high-profile political corruption investigations of RS and Federation political leaders to entity prosecutors' offices, which dismissed the cases and ended the investigations for lack of evidence.

Whistleblower Protection: In October the state-level parliament passed the Whistleblowers' Protection Law. The law provides protections for individuals employed in state-level public institutions who report corruption. There is no such law for the private sector.

Financial Disclosure: Candidates for high-level public office, including for parliament at the state and entity levels and for the Council of Ministers and entity government positions, are subject to financial disclosure laws. The Central Election Commission is responsible for ensuring compliance with the laws, which observers noted fell short of Organization for Economic Cooperation and Development and other international standards. Financial disclosure laws did not provide adequate investigative authority and enforcement mechanisms. Consequently, public officials and their relatives often declared only a fraction of their total assets and liabilities.

During the year authorities generally failed to make financial disclosure declarations public, ostensibly because of conflicts between the country's laws on financial disclosure and protection of personal information. There were criminal sanctions for noncompliance with financial disclosure laws, but authorities did not apply those sanctions during the year.

Public Access to Information: Although the law provides for citizen access to government records, many government agencies did not comply. Under the law the government must provide an explanation for any denial of access, and citizens may appeal denials in the court system or to the ombudsman's offices. The government sometimes failed to provide the required explanation for denial of access, but generally did so when citizens appealed denials through the ombudsman, courts, or legal aid. Public awareness of the law remained low.

Section 5. Governmental Attitude Regarding International and Nongovernmental Investigation of Alleged Violations of Human Rights

A variety of human rights groups and NGOs generally operated without restriction, investigating and publishing their findings on human rights cases. Government officials, however, were often inefficient and slow to respond to their views.

NGO participation in government decision-making processes varied by issue. Neither the government nor the NGO sector had sufficient knowledge of the mechanisms by which NGOs could participate in such processes. While the Council of Ministers can return draft legislation that has not undergone consultation with NGOs, it has not employed this mechanism to date. The Council of Ministers largely excluded NGOs from politically important or sensitive decisions. NGOs continued, however, to expand cooperation with the government at lower levels. In 2012 in addition to an agreement on cooperation signed by the Council of Ministers, more than 100 municipalities, approximately two-thirds of all municipalities in the country, and three cantons drafted and signed agreements with local NGOs.

According to a survey supported by the EU Commission, there were 13,000 NGOs registered in the country. Financial viability remained the most challenging obstacle for civil society organizations. Organizations that were not viewed as threats to governing parties mostly received support from local governments. Procedures to register or change an NGO's organizational statute took significantly longer than prescribed by law due to official inefficiency.

In April the state-level House of Representatives prohibited a representative of the Center of Civic Initiatives (CCI) from observing the body's session, alleging that the group's sources of financing were not transparent. The CCI viewed the measure as retaliation for the NGO's having published several critical reviews of parliament's work. The House of Representatives eventually allowed the CCI to resume its observation activity but with less access than it had before.

Public support mechanisms and regulations regarding NGOs were underdeveloped. Instead of following set guidelines and criteria, government commissions that allocated public funds appeared to base many of their decisions on political interests and allocated large percentages of funds to predetermined beneficiaries, such as religious communities, sports organizations, and veterans associations. The methods of allocation remained nontransparent and subject to corruption.

UN and Other International Bodies: The RS government was less responsive and cooperative than the state and Federation governments in dealing with the Office of the High Representative, which has special powers over the government under the Dayton Accords as affirmed by multiple UN Security Council resolutions and other international organizations, such as the ICRC, the International Commission on Missing Persons, and the OSCE.

Government Human Rights Bodies: The state-level ombudsman has authority to investigate violations of the country's human rights laws on behalf of individual citizens and to submit recommendations to the government for remedy. The ombudsman's recommendations are not legally binding.

The state-level parliament has a Joint Commission for Human Rights, Rights of Children, Youth, Immigration, Refugees, Asylum, and Ethics consisting of members of both houses of parliament. The 11-member commission participated in human rights-related activities with governmental and nongovernmental organizations.

Section 6. Discrimination, Societal Abuses, and Trafficking in Persons

The law prohibits discrimination based on race, gender, disability, language, sexual orientation, or social status; however, the government did not enforce these prohibitions effectively.

Women

Rape and Domestic Violence: Rape and spousal rape are illegal; the maximum penalty for either crime is 15 years' imprisonment. A sense of shame among rape victims and the failure of police to treat spousal rape as a serious offense inhibited the effective enforcement of the law. Consequently, rape, particularly spousal rape, often was unreported by victims and underreported by authorities. During the year the state-level Agency for Gender Equality, in cooperation with respective gender centers in the RS and the Federation, published research on the prevalence of abuse against women in the country. Research indicated almost half of the women surveyed experienced psychological or physical abuse from the age of 15 on. The most frequent form of abuse was psychological with a prevalence rate of 42 percent during ones' lifetime. The second most prevalent form of abuse was physical violence with a prevalence rate of 24 percent; the third most prevalent form of abuse was sexual violence with a prevalence rate of 6 percent.

The country undertook several initiatives to combat rape and domestic violence, but women did not fully use the protections available under the law because of a lack of knowledge and reluctance to use them. The Agency for Gender Equality reported that only 17 percent of women who experienced some form of domestic violence sought help. For example, while laws in both entities allow for the perpetrator to be removed from the home, this provision was rarely, if ever, enforced, since law enforcement officials were often under the mistaken impression that they needed to concern themselves with where the perpetrator would live. As a result women in danger were compelled to go to safe houses.

Violence against women, including domestic violence and sexual assault, remained widespread and underreported. According to NGO estimates, one-third of the women in the country were victims of domestic violence. Laws in both entities require police to remove an offender from the family home. NGOs reported that authorities, especially in the RS where domestic violence is a misdemeanor, often returned offenders to their family homes less than 24 hours later. In the Federation authorities had discretion to prosecute domestic violence as either a felony or a misdemeanor. Experts estimated that only 10 percent of domestic violence victims reported the crime.

Although police received specialized training in handling cases of domestic violence, NGOs reported a widespread reluctance among police in both entities to break up families by arresting offenders.

Social services agencies tended to be underfunded, understaffed, and undertrained in helping victims effectively. Filling this void were a multitude of NGOs dedicated to assisting victims of domestic violence, eight of which formed a strong cooperative network called Safe Network. This network developed two hotlines, one for each entity, which women could call when they needed services but were reluctant to contact police. The hotlines take an estimated 6,000 calls annually. Eight safe houses throughout the country received financial and other material support from the government during the year. Many of these doubled as shelters for trafficking victims.

Sexual Harassment: The law prohibits sexual harassment, but it was a serious problem. Many NGOs reported that victims almost never filed complaints because they did not recognize their experiences as harassment and were not aware of their legal rights.

Reproductive Rights: Couples and individuals have the right to decide freely and responsibly the number, spacing, and timing of their children and had the information and means to do so free from discrimination, coercion, and violence. There was easy access to contraception and skilled attendance during childbirth. Most women had access to prenatal and postpartum care through employer or government insurance.

Discrimination: Women have equal legal status to men, and authorities generally treated women equally. The government's Agency for Gender Equality worked to inform women of their rights. Women and men generally received equal pay for equal work at government-owned enterprises, but there were reports that the same was not true at private businesses. Women had problems with nonpayment of allowances for maternity leave and unwarranted dismissal of pregnant women and new mothers. Many job announcements openly advertised discriminatory criteria, such as age and physical appearance for female applicants. Women remained underrepresented in law enforcement agencies, although there was continued progress. The state- and entity-level parliaments had committees for gender equality.

Children

Birth registration: By law a child born to at least one citizen parent of the country is also a citizen, regardless of the place of birth. A child born on the territory of the country to noncitizen parents does not gain citizenship unless both parents are stateless persons, in which case they may apply for collective naturalization.

During the year the UNHCR, through a local legal aid NGO, registered the birth of children, mainly Roma, whose parents failed to register them. The NGO Vasa Prava estimated there were more than 4,000 unregistered children in the country. Unregistered children experienced significant obstacles in accessing government social, educational, and health benefits.

During the year a political dispute over implementation of a constitutional ruling affecting the law on issuance of personal identification numbers led to a three-month period in which there was no legal framework for issuing the numbers, which are required for obtaining social services and documents. The RS and Brcko District began issuing their own numbers, allegedly in coordination with the state-level agency. A newborn girl who needed a passport to go to Germany for medical treatment was denied a passport due to lack of an identification number. The child could not leave the country for treatment, and her health deteriorated. This case prompted the June protests outside parliament.

Child Abuse: Family violence against children was a problem. Police investigated and prosecuted individual cases of child abuse. The country's Agency for Gender Equality estimated that one in five families experienced domestic violence. Municipal centers for social work protected children's rights but lacked resources and housing for children who had fled abuse or who needed to be removed from abusive homes.

Forced and Early Marriage: The legal minimum age for marriage is 18 or 16 with parental consent. In certain Romani communities, girls married between the ages of 12 and 14. Children's rights and antitrafficking activists noted that prosecutors were reluctant to investigate and prosecute arranged marriages involving Romani minors on the grounds that such marriages were "their way." The government did not have any programs that specifically targeted reducing the incidence of child marriage. According to UNICEF statistics, 6 percent of women were married or in a union before they were 18 years of age.

Sexual Exploitation of Children: State-level penalties for sexual exploitation of children are up to 10 years in prison. Courts may sentence defendants to a total of 20 years under certain aggravating circumstances. At the entity level the penalties range from three to 15 years' imprisonment. Entity-level laws against "enticement to prostitution" permit police to treat minors who are 14 and older as "juvenile prostitutes" instead of victims of rape or trafficking in persons. Women's and children's rights NGOs complained that the law allows police to subject children who are between the ages of 14 and 17 to interrogation and criminal proceedings, although no such prosecutions were documented during the year. Under entity criminal codes, abuse of a child or juvenile for pornography is a crime that carries a sentence of one to five years' imprisonment. Authorities generally enforced these laws.

International Child Abductions: The country is a party to the 1980 Hague Convention on the Civil Aspects of International Child Abduction. For country-specific information see http://travel.state.gov/abduction/country/country_5974.html.

Anti-Semitism

There were no reports of anti-Semitic violence against members of the Jewish community, which authorities estimated to be fewer than 1,000 persons. Additionally, the 2013 edition of the standard Serb Orthodox textbook (*Pravoslavna Vjeronauka*, Banja Luka), authorized by the RS Ministry of Education for sixth graders, no longer contains anti-Semitic text.

Trafficking in Persons

See the Department of State's *Trafficking in Persons Report* at www.state.gov/j/tip.

Persons with Disabilities

The law in both entities and at the state level prohibits discrimination against persons with physical, sensory, intellectual, and mental disabilities in employment; education; access to health care, air travel, and other transportation; and the provision of other state services. There was, however, discrimination against persons with disabilities in these areas.

In the Federation the law provides that public buildings must be retrofitted to provide access to persons with disabilities and that new buildings also must be accessible. Buildings were rarely accessible to persons with disabilities, however. The RS has comparable laws for public access, but few older public buildings were accessible. Human rights NGOs complained that many new public buildings continued to be built without access for persons with disabilities.

Human rights NGOs complained that the government ineffectively implemented laws and programs to provide access to information.

The law requires children with disabilities to attend regular classes, but schools were often unable to accommodate them. Children with disabilities either attended classes using regular curricula in regular schools or attended schools for children with disabilities. Parents of children with disabilities, especially of those with extensive disabilities, faced many obstacles and authorities left them almost completely on their own to provide education for their children, although a growing number of programs for children with disabilities were available in schools.

National/Racial/Ethnic Minorities

The country's minorities experienced problems with discrimination in employment, occupation, and education in both the government and private sectors. While the law prohibits discrimination, human rights activists frequently complained that authorities did not adequately enforce the law.

Harassment and discrimination against minorities, often related to property disputes, continued throughout the country. Examples included desecration of graves, graffiti, arson and vandalism of houses of worship and other religious sites, verbal harassment, dismissal from work, threats, and physical assaults.

Violence and acts of intimidation against ethnic minorities often were directed at symbols and buildings of that minority's predominant religion. For more information, see the Department of State's *International Religious Freedom Report* at www.state.gov/j/drl/irf/rpt.

During the year the Herzegovina-Neretva Canton Court in Mostar struck down a decision by the Mostar Municipal Court that the "two schools under one roof" policy was discriminatory because the petitioners did not have legal standing to file the case. This decision effectively perpetuated the segregation of Bosniak and Croat primary school children in the regions of Stolac and Capljina. The Mostar Municipal Court's decision called for a single curriculum across all regions of the municipality. In a similar verdict, the Municipal Court of Travnik ruled against a lawsuit by the NGO Vasa Prava that also argued that the "two schools" policy was discriminatory.

Human rights activists noted that many textbooks reinforced stereotypes of the country's ethnic groups and that others missed opportunities to dispel stereotypes by excluding any mention of some ethnic groups, particularly Jews and Roma. State- and entity-level officials generally did not act to prevent such discrimination.

The University of Mostar remained divided into two separate institutions, reflecting the continued ethnic divide in the city. Parochial interests influenced the remaining five public universities in various ethnic-majority areas.

There were an estimated 80,000 to 100,000 Roma in the country. Some Romani leaders reported an increase in Romani emigration and asylum-seeking abroad during the year due to discrimination in access to social benefits. Roma experienced discrimination in access to housing, health care, education, and employment opportunities. The Roma Information Council estimated that only 1 percent of working-age Roma were employed and indicated that employers usually fired Roma first during a reduction in force. Roma were underrepresented in public sector employment, despite constitutional provisions for proportional representation in public institutions; the problem in part was the result of old census data that underreported the size of the Romani population.

Many Roma lacked birth certificates, identification cards, or a registered residence, preventing them from accessing health care and public education services or registering to vote. Many Roma, especially those displaced during the 1992-95 war, lived in informal settlements that often lacked access to basic services. School enrollment for Romani children was below the national average. There were credible reports that Romani students were overrepresented in special schools for children with intellectual disabilities.

In accordance with the Roma Decade of Inclusion, the state-level government in May revised its Roma National Action Plan for housing, employment, and health care. The government allocated approximately 650,000 convertible marks ($1 million) annually to finance the action plan. To date, some 212 Romani families benefited from government employment programs, 360 families have received housing assistance, and 270 families benefited from infrastructure improvements in their communities.

Many human rights NGOs criticized law enforcement authorities for widespread indifference toward Romani victims of domestic violence and human trafficking.

Societal Abuses, Discrimination, and Acts of Violence Based on Sexual Orientation and Gender Identity

While state-level law prohibits discrimination on the basis of sexual orientation, it was not fully enforced, and there was frequent societal discrimination against LGBT persons. Although state-level laws provide protections to LGBT persons, a gap in entity-level laws left room for discrimination by allowing subnational law enforcement to deflect responsibility for crimes based on sexual orientation.

LGBT persons faced frequent harassment and discrimination, including termination of employment. In some cases dismissal letters explicitly stated that sexual orientation was the cause of termination, making it extremely difficult for them to find another job. In its 2013 report on rights and freedoms of LGBT persons, the Sarajevo Open Center noted that most state-level institutions assume that the prohibition of discrimination regulated by state-level law is sufficient to protect LGBT persons. At the same time, entity level laws do not provide explicit protections to LGBT persons.

In March attackers verbally and physically abused seven members of the LGBT rights organization Okvirin Sarajevo near the presidency building. Following the incident, a special riot police unit arrived at the scene to collect names and details, but police never issued a formal report or made any arrests. The unidentified attackers, a group of 18 to25 males, remained at large at year's end.

In May, Mayor Marko Pavic of Prijedor referred to the May 31 commemoration known as the Day of White Armbands, which honors persons killed in the municipality during the 1992-95 conflict, as a "gay pride parade." Several activist organizations stated that Pavic's remarks insulted not only the victims of the conflict but members of the LGBT community as well. The RS Helsinki Committee for Human Rights issued an immediate condemnation of Pavic's statement and the director of communications at the International Center for Transitional Justice criticized Pavic's "continuous policy of discrimination."

Other Societal Violence or Discrimination

There was significant social stigma and employment discrimination against persons with HIV/AIDS, as well as a low level of public understanding of the nature of the infection. The government lacked properly trained counselors and a systematic method of referring persons with HIV/AIDS for outside counseling. Authorities often relied on periodic, informal requests from the NGO Apoha to relay contact information to persons whose doctors had recently diagnosed them with HIV/AIDS. During the year the Interreligious Council, composed of representatives of all four of the country's major religious communities, continued a public campaign to reduce prejudice against persons with HIV/AIDS.

Promotion of Acts of Discrimination

There were widespread comments in the media and public discourse designed to paint members of other ethnic groups in negative terms, usually in relation to the 1992-95 war. During the year the RS president and senior officials in his political party, as well as other officials and leaders in the RS, repeatedly denied that Serb forces committed genocide at Srebrenica in 1995, despite the findings of multiple local and international courts.

Section 7. Worker Rights

a. Freedom of Association and the Right to Collective Bargaining

The law provides for the right of workers in both entities (including migrant workers, but excluding members of the military) to form and join independent unions and bargain collectively. In both entities and the Brcko District, the law provides for the right to strike. In the Federation the law has burdensome requirements for workers who wish to conduct a strike. Trade unions cannot officially announce a strike without first reaching an agreement with the employer on which "essential" personnel would remain at work. If no agreement is reached, the strike may be declared illegal. This provision effectively allowed employers to prevent legitimate strikes. The law prohibits antiunion discrimination.

The government did not effectively enforce all applicable laws. Authorities did not impose sanctions against employers who prevented workers from organizing. Violations of worker rights continued to be a lower priority for ministry inspectors, as state officials instead focused on bolstering state revenues by cracking down on unregistered employees and employers who did not pay taxes. Some unions reported that employers threatened employees with dismissal if they joined a union and in some cases fired union leaders for their activities.

The labor inspectorates and courts did not deal effectively with complaints of antiunion discrimination by employers, although Federation and RS courts often ruled in favor of workers in union-related disputes. The government did not impose fines on employers who prevented workers from unionizing. While no legal or technical barriers prevent an employee from bringing a complaint against an employer, high unemployment coupled with fear of losing one's job, a backlogged court system, and the lack of legal protection for the approximately 20 percent of the labor force working in the informal economy were disincentives to filing complaints. Employers also complained of the long and tedious court process that was invoked if an employee alleged unjust dismissal.

Workers exercised their right to join a union and bargain collectively, and unions were generally independent from the government and political parties. The respective governments and representative organizations of employers and workers in both entities negotiated general collective agreements fixing conditions of work. A number of private employers refused to recognize these agreements. Labor authorities in the Federation noted that employers and workers often did not fully consider whether such agreements were financially sustainable when they were signed. Trade union representatives alleged that antiunion discrimination was widespread in all districts.

After 10 years before the state court, the Trade Union of Bosnia and Herzegovina won its case against the state minister of justice and was registered in May 2012. Since 2002 the government had not allowed the union, which represented approximately 260,000 workers, primarily from Federation government-owned enterprises, to register as a union at the state level. Lack of formal recognition had blocked the union from engaging in dialogue on labor problems pertaining to state-level competencies with partners.

b. Prohibition of Forced or Compulsory Labor

While the law prohibits all forms of forced or compulsory labor, the government at times did not enforce these laws effectively. There were reports that individuals and organized crime syndicates sometimes trafficked women and children for begging and forced labor (see section 7.c.). During the year "day centers" working in cooperation with the country's antitrafficking coordinator in Banja Luka, Zenica, and Tuzla provided services to 725 at-risk children. The day centers focused primarily on children who were especially vulnerable to forced begging. In January the municipal court of Kalesija sentenced Malenko Marinkovic to two years' imprisonment after he admitted holding a 19-year-old woman for 11 years in domestic servitude.

Also see the Department of State's *Trafficking in Persons Report* at www.state.gov/j/tip.

c. Prohibition of Child Labor and Minimum Age for Employment

The minimum age for employment of children in both entities is 15; minors between the ages of 15 and 18 must provide a valid health certificate to work. The RS and Brcko District have laws that penalize employers for hiring persons younger than 15. The Federation is in the process of adopting a similar law. The labor codes of the Federation, the RS, and the Brcko District also prohibit minors between the ages of 15 and 18 from working at night and performing hazardous labor, although the Federation's labor code does not define hazardous labor. The labor codes in the RS and Brcko do define hazardous labor.

Entity governments are responsible for enforcing child labor laws, and both entities and the Brcko District enforced them. During the year the government neither received nor investigated any reports of child labor at places of employment. Neither entity had inspectors dedicated to child labor inspections; authorities investigated violations of child labor laws as part of a general labor inspection. Both entities' labor inspectorates reported that they found no significant violations of child labor laws although they did not conduct reviews of children working on family farms. The government did not collect data on child labor.

Also see the Department of Labor's *Findings on the Worst Forms of Child Labor* at www.dol.gov/ilab/programs/ocft/tda.htm.

d. Acceptable Conditions of Work

The monthly minimum wage in the Federation was 350 convertible marks ($240). In the RS, the monthly minimum wage was 361 convertible marks ($250), except in the textile and footwear sectors, where it was 313 convertible marks ($220). The Brcko District did not have a separate minimum wage or an independent pension fund, and employers typically used the minimum wage rate of the entity to which its workers decided to direct their pension funds. The World Bank estimated approximately 48 percent of the population lived below the poverty line.

The legal workweek in both entities and the Brcko District is 40 hours, although seasonal workers may work up to 60 hours. The law limits overtime to 10 hours per week in both entities. An employee in the RS may legally volunteer for an additional 10 hours of overtime in exceptional circumstances. The Federation has no provision for premium pay, while the RS requires a 30 percent premium. Laws in both entities require a minimum rest period of 30 minutes during the workday.

Employers in each entity and the Brcko District must provide a minimum of nine paid annual holidays. Employees may choose which holidays to observe depending on ethnic or religious affiliation. Entity labor laws prohibit excessive compulsory overtime. RS law holds employers responsible for improving working conditions. Entity labor laws set mandatory occupational health and safety standards, especially for those industry sectors in which there were hazardous working conditions for workers. Worker rights extended to all official (i.e., registered) workers, including migrant and temporary ones.

The entities and the Brcko District did little to enforce regulations on working hours, daily and weekly rest, or annual leave, and these protections were generally believed to be lacking.

The Federation Market Inspectorate, the RS Inspectorate, and the Brcko District Inspectorate are responsible for enforcement related to work conditions. There were 79 market inspectors in the Federation, 41 in the RS, and 11 in the Brcko District. Authorities in both entities and the Brcko District did not adequately enforce regulations related to work conditions. While labor inspectorates made some effort to enforce registration of employees, they limited most inspections to conditions affecting the officially registered workforce.

During the year governments in both entities made some limited efforts to improve working conditions at government-owned coal mines by purchasing newer equipment. Workers in certain industries, particularly metal and steel processing and coal mining, often worked in hazardous conditions. According to informal estimates, approximately 40 percent of the total work force was unregistered and in the informal economy. The entity labor ministries did not maintain official statistics on workplace fatalities and injuries. During the year there were no major industrial accidents. There were no official social protections for workers in the informal economy.

www.ingramcontent.com/pod-product-compliance
Lightning Source LLC
Chambersburg PA
CBHW080742290526
45790CB00008B/3293